D0332188

Dearest Merrie,

may your life be ensouled
with messages from the
oracle —
    every day
        every way
            always.

With love & gratitude,

    Caryl Ann

THE
EVERYWHERE
ORACLE

A GUIDED JOURNEY THROUGH POETRY
FOR AN ENSOULED WORLD

CARYL ANN CASBON

Wyatt-MacKenzie Publishing
DEADWOOD, OREGON

The Everywhere Oracle
A Guided Journey Through Poetry for an Ensouled World

by Caryl Ann Casbon

ISBN: 978-1-942545-08-8 Paperback
Library of Congress Control Number: 2015940849

ALL RIGHTS RESERVED
©2015 Caryl Ann Casbon

"A Toast to an Empty Garage" is based on a version
previously published by "Weavings."

All trademarks are the property of their respective owners.

Wyatt-MacKenzie Publishing, Inc.
www.WyattMacKenzie.com

Wyatt-MacKenzie Publishing
DEADWOOD, OREGON

Publisher's Cataloging-in-Publication data

Casbon, Caryl Ann.
   The Everywhere oracle : a guided journey through poetry for an ensouled world/
Caryl Ann Casbon.
   pages cm
   ISBN 978-1-942545-08-0
   Includes index and bibliographical references.

1. Poetry. 2. Spirituality —Poetry. 3. Poetry —Handbooks, manuals, etc. I. Title.

PS303 .375 2015
811.6 —dc23   2015940849

Dedication

I dedicate this book to Jesse John Casbon (aka the Holy Rascal),
my husband and soul partner, my everyday Oracle,
who knows how to live with his hand on the Wire,
and share with me the ever-unfolding adventure of
coming alive to this wondrous journey called life.

And...

To Maryellen Kelley, my spiritual mother and friend, who recently
transitioned to More Life: Cherishments galore to you for your living
example of how to embody God's rascally-free nature and radical
abundance of outpouring love that is yearning to dance in us,
through us, among us, always. Maryellen, what a "soul tail-wager"
and inspiration you will always be in my heart.

Praise for *The Everywhere Oracle*

"Listening to and lifting up the human soul has been my life-work, and I know the power of poetry to speak the soul's voice. So I opened Caryl Ann Casbon's *The Everywhere Oracle* with high expectations, all of which were fulfilled. Caryl's poems contain strong storylines, humor, lovely turns of irony, questions and colorful metaphors that offer windows into her soul while simultaneously inviting readers to explore their own.

Original, deceptively simple, and easily accessible, these poems celebrate the mysterious unfolding of the inner life and point towards the guidance, clarity and meaning to be found in our everyday encounters. The Reader's Guide at the back of the book extends that celebration beyond the individual reader to fellow seekers, offering people a way to be in soulful community with each other at a time when so many are hungry for exactly that experience."

> — **Parker J. Palmer**, Author of *Let Your Life Speak, The Courage to Teach, A Hidden Wholeness,* and *Healing the Heart of Democracy*

"Behind the screen of the modern world, under the veneer of our digital distractions, in spite of planes and cars and phones, there is a world of holy wells and hidden stories, prophecies waiting for your listening. This book offers readers a succession of opening doors to that realm of personal mystery, of patient revelation. Will you open it? A story that could be buried—or blessed. An episode of struggle that could be hidden—or cherished as personal scripture. These are the choices that will be yours as you enter this book of ordinary epiphanies. That's just it: treasures of understanding wait in plain sight, but you may need this guide."

> — **Kim Stafford**, NW poet, Author of *The Muses Among Us: Eloquent Listening and Other Pleasures of the Writer's Craft*

The Everywhere Oracle

"Calling *The Everywhere Oracle* a book is rather a misnomer. It is more like having a living, truthful, playful and wise storyteller in your presence! You will find Caryl Ann Casbon's poems dancing off the pages into your heart, awakening new dimensions to your experiences and world that perhaps were always close at hand but just out of reach. You will laugh and cry with her, and her self-compassionate honesty will inspire you to do the same. Caryl Ann's ensouling poems and her way of making them accessible through each chapter's introduction and reflection will nurture our great longing for the truly Intimate and the truly Real."

> — **Susan Plummer, Ph.D**, Author of *Deep Change: Befriending the Unknown*

"Caryl Casbon's book is a find for seekers of spiritual wisdom in secular life; its pages, a satisfying interplay of shadow and light. It is deeply personal, yet universal. The poems are pearls — each one is a beauty that stands alone. Strung together they elegantly encircle a life well lived. I look forward to sharing them with my clients."

> — **Nancy Ilene Gump, MFT**, Psychotherapist in San Francisco

"I am fortunate to be an early reader of Caryl Ann Casbon's poetry. From her writing workshops to her retreat settings, when she has shared her work, her poems have resonated deeply with me and I return to them often and use them in my own writing workshops and literature classrooms. Her poems sparkle with insight and wisdom, and often, her gentle humor. Caryl's poems are a true offering: accessible, yet with great depth that invite connections for the reader. Her poems are the kind likely to make fans out of her readers, as their subject matter deals with loss and difficult transitions, and also love and the many pleasures of the imagination.

I am grateful that she is generously offering to share her work more widely through this collection, and the added framework for those of us who choose to use them in group settings."

> — **Dr. Ruth Shagoury**, Endowed Chair, Lewis & Clark College, Author of *Living the Questions,* and 12 other books on literacy

Caryl Ann Casbon

Preface

$\mathcal{W}$hen I write poetry, I don't have a goal in mind other than to faithfully put pen to paper every day. The idea for a poem arrives out of the ether where I'm vaguely aware of noticing it. Gradually it acts like a lost dog tailing me, hoping for a handout. Ultimately, it won't leave me alone until I find it a home, give it a name, and nurture it with my wholehearted attention. In other words, my writing life lacks a strategic plan.

When I first attempted to pull these poems together for this book, I despaired at the absence of any obvious organizing principles. The poems were a bunch of orphan mutts gathered at the humane society, barking stridently in their own cages, not a family that might talk to each other. "Who are these poor hounds?" I asked.

Yet slowly two camps into which the poems might gather began to reveal themselves. Two themes emerged, which turned out to be close relations, a family camp if you will. They are the themes of change and the inner life. I shouldn't be surprised, for I have been obsessed with these matters for as long as I can remember.

Then, when writing the poem, "The Oracle Everywhere," another insight christened a larger theme that became the container for the two primary threads in this collection. That overarching theme is one that the Oracle is alive everywhere! It turns out that engaging in an ongoing dialogue with Great Mystery is not only possible, but is all pervasive! If we attune, it has a great deal to say to us in so many surprising ways, which may seem random, unrelated, and even outrageous when they show up, yet all evidence points to the fact that we live in a world and universe that is "en-souled" with meaning, guidance, and love that are Divine in nature, yet personal in translation. Really. I am not making this up. I know, however, that accepting this to be true is different than experiencing it yourself.

My mentor and dear Oracle-friend, Maryellen Kelley, said to me, "You know, Caryl Ann, these poems aren't for you." Well, I didn't know that, but I did listen. This book is an offering, one I hope you can use in a way that makes the poems specifically "for you." But, it does involve a little work.

There is an immense difference between simply reading a poem for its first impressions versus entering into a relationship with it. So many people say, "I have a hard time with poetry. It's not accessible." I know what they mean. Yet when you engage in conversation with a poem, it has the potential for touching you on a soul level. It can challenge you, speak to you, and invite you into a dialogue with your own inner teacher. It is in this way it can become a poem for you. When approached like this, there is no right or wrong way to interpret poetry. It is for you to discover its unique meaning for your life, in spite of what your literature professor told you in college!

I have a deep respect for questions. Asking powerful, timely, clear questions is an art and a finely honed skill. I believe that the quality of our lives depends on the quality of questions we ask and take seriously. The right question can change the course of your life. An insightful question can open you to your inner Oracle, the voice of your soul. Now that is pure gold.

In the spirit of creating "access points" to my poems, I've crafted some questions to accompany them. These questions are intended to engage you in a conversation, but if they don't work for you, listen for the ones that bubble up from within and respond to them instead!

If you are interested in exploring these poems in a book club, church group, women's or men's group, etc., there are instructions for a group design in the Appendix. And of course, you can just read the poems and take what you will from them. But, I do confess to a prejudice. I think you will have a deeper experience if you journal and reflect on them in some way.

May you read these poems in a way that puts you in touch with the Oracle within you, around you and entirely surrounding this exquisite world Everywhere you look!

~ Caryl Ann Casbon, Bend, Oregon

Caryl Ann Casbon

TABLE OF CONTENTS

CHAPTER ONE
Where Time Is Calling You Now
The Alchemy of Change

CHAPTER TWO
To Live Inside an Ancient Rhythm
Poems for the Inner Life

CHAPTER ONE

Where Time Is Calling You Now: The Alchemy of Change

I admit I have a love/hate relationship with change. My partner tells me I am not very good at it. We recently moved from a home of 13 years during which time we buried Tucker, our favorite Maine Coon cat of all time, and both of my parents, secured and left my last real organizational position, and watched our daughter pack off to college. Like the old, torn pink comfort blanket I dragged around as a child, I emotionally clung to that home until the day we moved, even though its time in our lives was used up, kaput. It was embarrassing, really. We say we want to change, but deep down, often fight it all the way. In retrospect, every new home we've moved into has been a significant improvement over the one left behind. Will I ever learn?

I like my routines too, yet they can be obstacles to change. Have you ever interrupted a cat taking a bath? If you intrude on them in the midst of their cleansing ritual, they get an annoyed, puzzled look on their faces, pause, then pick up right where they left off until they rough-tongue clean themselves to the bitter end. Ah, the power of homeostasis.

Still, I've studied the dynamics of change for many years. I'm fairly certain they hold the alchemical secrets to transformation. Robert Bosnak notes in his work on alchemy, that psychologists who have long studied the ancient practice of alchemy find remarkable parallels between the ways alchemists transformed metals into gold, and how the human psyche individuates and transforms the soul. The alchemists' work required patience, courage, and an ongoing regimen of questioning what was happening. There was recognition that to approach this Mystery, they must be related to, and dependent upon a Transpersonal Presence, and thus always began their work with prayer. As we approach change in our lives with this level of rigorous reverence and attention, all kinds of surprising chemistry is possible.

As alchemists, or guardians of the Mysteries of change, we seek the Holy in the midst of disruptions, loss and transition, especially when it is painful, for therein lies the gold. While not all change means growth, there is no growth without change. It's everywhere, really, built into our bodies, life-cycles, the seasons, each day, the patterns in nature: birth, growth, decline, death, and rebirth. In this universe, nothing stands still. If you are human you live and breathe change. It's so prevalent it is easy to miss.

While there are many facets to change, these poems coalesce into three areas: Inheritance, The Crossroads of Change, and Change Across the Lifecycle, as described below. So, here is an invitation to you, to look closely and question the alchemy of change in your life through the mirror of these poems and short essays.

Section I: Inheritance
These poems offer different perspectives to some of the
dimensions of these "inheritances."

Section II: The Crossroads of Change
These poems explore ways to avoid, befriend, tend to,
and even embrace our deepest needs
for change and growth.

Section III: Change Across the Lifecycle
These poems invite you to explore your relationship with
your progression of years and the changes that result,
regardless of what age you are.

My sincerest wish is that these poems speak to you,
to your soul and your evolutionary relationship
to the alchemy of change, close-up.

Inheritance

*S*ome of the most difficult things to change in my life started very young, even before birth or memory, when I was not conscious of their formation. These poems explore some of the dimensions of these "inheritances."

A Toast to an Empty Garage

In Germany, at least once a year
a bomb explodes under the Autobahn
where the vibration of wheels activate its timing device,
or near schools, injuring children playing soccer in fields.
A full-time bomb squad still searches for these deadly remnants,
bombs dropped and buried from a war, now 70 years past.
You would think it would be over by now.
Forgotten.
It's not.

It is said that every object has a vibration,
a frequency with an energetic field.
Like the lost bombs of WWII,
my garage stores old family heirlooms: a vanity from Aunt Alice's
bedroom contains the memory of her miserable marriage to
Uncle Dick,
collects dust, incubates their suffering, leaking upward
through the heat vents.

Clutter zones of ancestral histories pile up, underground:
cut glass liquor decanters from my parents' alcohol-infused
post-war union—
endless, four-cocktail evenings in front of the T.V. set.
Eight antique glasses from Aunt Betty, now with Spirit,
who generously gifted us, saying:
"Don't ever put these in the dishwasher or lose them.
They are very valuable."

I lift one of the glasses up in the darkness of the garage
in an offering, a sacred toast.
"To Betty: thank you for your generosity."
Silently ask for her forgiveness as I wrap the glasses in newspaper
for Goodwill. "I love your love,
but these glasses have to go.
They are ugly and we don't use them.

They are dragging us down. Amen."
Feng Shui, the 3,000-year-old Taoist art and science
of the material world, which is the spirit world.
What is without is within.
Keep what is current for you,
which keeps you in the current,
and brings you Light.
Release what is old, pulls you backwards,
 is used up, or should be.

Cull your life, and see what freedom
you may find in an empty garage.

Hunger: Where Can't Turns to Want

Mom didn't like to talk about the past.
One story survived from The Great Depression,
about the time Grandma hocked her wedding ring to buy
her a prom dress after standing in line for free cabbage.

A nutrition major, Mom dropped out of UCLA
to care for Grandpa who slowly died from alcoholism.
It erased him from family memory
like the Red Sea swallowed up Pharaoh's army.
I don't even know what he looked like.

Later, no longer poor,
her mantra, "I'm fat," droned a constant refrain,
a self-imposed cycle of scarcity set for life.
Drawing battle lines around the cookie tin,
she guarded it like the bank.
"Dessert will make you chubby,"
still sings in my head, where can't turns to want.

When I was eight, I snuck a can of peanuts,
devoured the whole thing crouched behind the incinerator,
then claimed, "I didn't do it."
I can still feel the dread, fear of punishment,
the deep poverty of my actions.

Eating, so elemental, maternal,
deformed at conception, grown in the soil
ancestral trauma, world wars and the Great Depression.

A college friend, dying from stomach cancer,
whispered to me words that haunt:
"At least I am finally skinny."
Words that make me weep.
Will I, too, take this weight to my grave?

Caryl Ann Casbon

The Year I Gave Up Alcohol

Like hermit crabs, addictions are resourceful
impersonators hidden in vacated snail shells,
protecting soft bodies in borrowed homes.

Not sure if it was an addiction or habit,
I swore off alcohol, thought, "Well,
I just drink on special occasions."
Turns out that was the first soft lie.
Where I live, we drink wine at
First Fridays, mid-week book signings,
5:00 p.m. drop-ins, to celebrate vacations,
holidays, weddings, funerals, communion.
Turns out, there is a special occasion almost every night.

I thought, "I don't really need it," the second lie.
Turns out, it works pretty well, masks
social anxiety, insecurity, edgy feelings, a hidden hunger.
Life's a little raw without it, most nights.
It disguises what my soft body is trying to voice,
that I'm tired, or don't like that person,
or regret my own behavior, or
just want to be alone.

I thought, "I won't miss it,"
the third lie. I do.

I believed, "Stop drinking, be free of compulsion."
Turns out the crab deftly
sidled into the closest shell, food, hard-wired to muffle
my own darkness just waiting to roar.
Turns out it's really hard to get to the bottom of this.

I learned a few things in my year without alcohol.
The hermit crab's shell conceals a vulnerable creature living in the dark,
afraid to show itself, become prey.

It needs a home but has settled for a shell.
It will come out, but only when you go down
to where it lives, look deeply into its buggy eyes,
then let it speak truth to your soul
about life without a shell.
Turns out it is here you find the place where
the Ocean holds you,
where longing is no more.

One Generation Off the Farm

They say most of us are one generation off the farm.
My dad, youngest of 10 in his family of Swedish emigrants,
hitchhiked from South Dakota to LA when
grasshoppers devoured the first successful crop in 12 years,
aged Grandpa 10 years in a day.

I sometimes work in Saskatchewan
where the prairies offer the eye distances,
where dreams haunt with
the howls of wolves, sounds of ancient hollow drums.
It's so cold in winter car tires freeze in squares;
in the short, sweltering summers
ticks hide in grasses, invade private parts.

Stories abound of moose that romance the horses,
charge cars in passionate territorial fury,
or the infamous cow that went feral,
survived many sub-zero winters in the deep woods;
no handsome bull could lure her out.

The women don't dye their hair, put on five pounds each winter,
at 50, look 60, worn by the elements.
They don't complain, share wildly funny stories
that run in their blood.

I feel oddly at home here, sense the prairies hold a secret
to something lost before I was born,
the farmer DNA hidden deep in my bones.
I might stop wearing makeup if I lived here.

One Easter, I noticed a cross on a hilltop in deep snow
draped with a purple sash blowing in the wind.
A father treks up there every holy week with the local priest,
prays for his son and wife run down on their snowmobile
by a truck on an icy road. He watched helplessly nearby.

The whole town knows them, speaks with hushed respect
for the family, the father, the ever-present danger,
the hardships that hold them close
in the raw, relentless prairie winds.

Perhaps we pay too high a price for our comfortable lives.
Perhaps we should spend time on the northern Canadian prairies,
apprentice ourselves to their fierce beauty.

The Crossroads of Change

*W*hat inspires us to change? Isn't homeostasis more comfortable? We are quite stealthy at avoiding change, and usually wait until we are uncomfortable to alter our course, for change often demands that we look at our shadows, wake up, give up coveted security, and learn. In these poems I explore my ways of negotiating change, whether it is dredging up wounds that require tending that are inhibiting my growth, or paying heed to some of the inner warning lights that something is wrong: boredom, depression, anger, low morale. The paradox is that the more we resist these symptoms, the stronger they grow; the more we befriend them, the greater the potential for something new. Like a fresh wound on your arm, the instinct is to not touch it, yet to heal, the injury needs tending. These poems explore ways to avoid, befriend, tend to, and even embrace our deepest needs for change and growth:

- God's Holy Mirrors
- The Dummy's Guide to Outsourcing Morale
- The Harm Reduction Program
- Crossroads of the Emergent Self
- The Four Directions for an Awakening Edge
- From the Perspective of Eternity
- The Final Carry-on

God's Holy Mirrors

Ireland shelters over 3,000 artesian wells
bubbling up in the barrens, fields, cow pastures,
some pilgrimage sites named for saints.
The wells offer thin places to seek healing,
to cleanse sorrows.

Tradition teaches pilgrims
to first dip strips of cloth into the holy well water
to bathe the wound, then hang them
in branches of nearby trees to air in the wind.
Next, circle and circle the well's dark, cold waters,
seven times,
in the direction of the sun
seeking illumination.

When you thirst, and draw up cold water with a bucket
from the depths,
you might catch a glimpse of your shadow
in your own reflection.
Then, you drink from the living waters of self-knowledge,
however cold and painful to swallow.

Sometimes pilgrims return year after year
with the same injury, until eventually they are ready
to hear its hidden message. Now they can depart for home,
the wound's scar a reminder of the hard-earned lesson
imprinted on their skin.

The Celts call Nature *God's First Bible*;
if that is the case, perhaps the wells are
God's Holy Mirrors.

Caryl Ann Casbon

A Dummy's Guide to Outsourcing Morale

A visiting friend recently noted
that morale is low
at the college where I used to work.
Administration is hiring a consultant
to work on it full-time.

The tenured professors skip
faculty meetings, miss office hours;
the dean calls for a "Strategic Plan!"
a year-long, time-sucking vortex of committee work creating
a document destined for a lonely long shelf-life.

Sounds like:
A Dummy's Guide to Outsourcing Morale:
A Sure-Fire Program for Avoidance of Growth.

Who can't understand this?
Who wants to endure the real work of low morale,
the descent to murky zones: poor leadership,
cynicism, disempowerment, low trust?
Our secret shame that maybe we created this?

I've tried to outsource
the hard labor of my inner life,
ignore the inconvenient nigglings of unhappiness,
disengagement, boredom,
called for strategic plans to help me power through:
self-help books, overeating—technologizing,
busyness, travel, motivational speakers.

The good news is they never work.

The warnings only increase until
I eventually face my own miserable state,
that my loved ones are not keeping office hours.

Then begin the real work,
ask difficult questions, endure their harsh truth,
obey their calls for change.
It is the only way back to aliveness,
but I still try to outsource it
whenever I can.

The Harm Reduction Program

I met this beautiful man
who leads Harm Reduction Programs
for the homeless.
Not grandiose recovery programs, with promises for salvation,
but harm reduction, doing less of that which damages.

Reminds me of how bumper stickers changed
from the 60s promoting a remedy for war:
Love One Another, decorated with large green peace signs,
to today's: **Coexist**, or **Tolerance**, written in symbols from
Christianity, Islam, and Judaism.
If we can't love one another, surely we can tolerate,
live at respectful distances? Do less harm.

I've spent a lifetime trying to recover
from my own violent tendencies
with about equal success as the 60s Peace Movement.
As lasting as band-aids under the shower,
the self-improvement slogans clog the drain
in my attempts to come clean.
Harm reduction is more of an inside job.

First, you must acknowledge why you want to do harm.
Then treat it like an abandoned feral kitten in the bushes:
bring it indoors, feed it warm milk,
hold its little wild banshee-like body close,
feel it in your heart, as a part of the fabric of who you are.
Give it a name.

Gradually, it stops scratching, spitting, running for cover,
starts a long relationship that one day might warm your lap
if you accept it may not be done with you, ever.
Then it can begin
to teach you about peace.

Crossroads of the Emergent Self

I departed for college an innocent,
Republican Christian ingénue,
bags crammed with dresses sewn
with my mother's love,
only to return home for Christmas vacation
braless, sporting overalls and agnostic leanings,
a Shape Shifting juncture when
growth, environment, and time
transformed me into a strange animal.
I forever walked differently in the world.

Like a molting parrot, feathers sticking out awkwardly,
bald spots showing, the emerging shape appeared
homely, awkward, unable to fly just yet.
A part of me yearned
to return to the graceful innocent swan I once was;
Mom and Dad considered putting this foreign bird
up for adoption.

It's happened many times now;
with each shifting of shapes life increased,
formed me into a more complex creature.
Just as shamans morph into
plants, animals, spheres of light to travel through space and time,
we transmute,
progress across Divine Intersections
opening to larger horizons.
Evolution, risk and hope meet at these crossroads
of the emergent self.

My friend, now at death's door,
looks back, tries to cling to her old plumage
as it molts away.
The Consummate Shape Shifter
strips her of her old feathers,

calls for surrender to the Faith of the Phoenix
on whose wings she will arise from the ashes,
like a sphere of light,
to travel through space beyond
the fires of this existence.

The Four Directions For An Awakening Edge

When a question haunts you, like:
What am I to do with the rest of my life?
and you're sincerely willing to let the answers
change you, surprise you
with what you don't already know,
then you are ready.

Awaken before dawn to face East,
the direction of the rising sun.
Bow down and pray for help.
Give thanks for the guidance you consent to follow,
then carry your question,
on this awakening edge,
into the new day.

Mid-morning, turn to the South.
Invoke the clarity of its direct exposure.
In this light, your question might change.
Be alert for omens.

At noon, face West.
Here, sort the fruits of the spirit,
when western exposure casts
long shadows across your path.
Ask questions that evoke...

What in my life wasn't harvested in time,
squandered like rotting apples blanketing
the orchard's floor?
What was picked too soon, remains hard,
green and unyielding?

What bursts with ripeness, ready to nourish, flourish?
What's overgrown in the soil of false rewards?

Caryl Ann Casbon
20

Here Intuition murmurs. Take notes.
Put your question down for an afternoon nap.
It takes time and ripening to birth wisdom into form.

Repeat the above as often as needed
until one evening, an answer arrives in an effervescent whisper.
Listen. You now know what you need to do.

Then, at twilight, turn to the North.
Open your arms wide to the setting sun;
watch your changed life
take wing like a flock of geese at dusk,
fluid in flight,
realized and released to the world.

Sunset songs celebrate creation anew,
then disappear into the dark.

From the Perspective of Eternity

Some Quaker Meetings don't appoint ministers,
instead listen for the Spark of the Divine within
to give voice through anyone, anytime.
They call this
the priesthood of all believers.
Imagine the democracy of that?

When a Friend fills up with Light
she quakes within,
a sign to let speech overflow into the room,
held ready in an expectant waiting silence.

On thresholds of great change, marriage,
heartbreaking loss, or enticing prospects,
they assemble a few allies, then,
for hours hold steady a candle
of faith to illuminate the emergent truth,
ask questions that evoke wisdom from within.

It's called a Clearness Committee,
where bearing reverent, questioning witness
serves the life and formation of another's soul.

When my mother died suddenly,
burdened with sadness from
a lifetime of misunderstanding, judgment,
I called such a committee to my hearth.
In the safe shelter of this circle,
a question eventually appeared:
*What would your mother say, now,
from the perspective of Eternity?*

Ah.

Caryl Ann Casbon

It was as though soft lights turned
on within the darkness of my grief,
dissolved into healing tears that cleansed my despair,
settled me at home in a new beginning with my mother.
A nonlocal perspective opened the way to
a love greater than death
through this simple, listening circle of kindred spirits.

I don't know what love is, really,
but in these committees,
divination is possible with
exquisite clearness, trust and attention.

The right question *can* change your life.

The Final Carry-on

I heard about a mortician who handed out
300 empty suitcases, then asked
they be filled with things to
be packed for the journey into death.
He displayed them in galleries and airports,
other crossroads of sorts,
inviting busy travelers to pause,
consider final destinations.

I know what I'll pack
for this journey
where there's no need for boarding passes
nor security screening delays.

I'll ride the last wave out on a surfboard,
wear a pair of dark glasses to handle the intense light.
Tuck my cat, Stewart, under my arm
to remind me to be like her, more curious than afraid.

I'll pack a telescope and iPhone
to spy on my dear ones left behind,
then text them: "I love you...I'm not far away at all."

I'd slip in a bottle of Windex
to wash clear any unfinished business
from the mirror of my old life,
plus eyeglasses for 20/20 vision
to see what it had all been about.

For the Welcoming Committee Picnic,
I'll load it up with Mom's favorite iceberg lettuce salad,
a box of See's Candy for Dad, and
a book about flying saucers for Grandma.

In my pocket, I'll hide a seashell that hums
ocean songs, sings praises of
Mother Earth's beauty.

Ultimately, I'll release this baggage to
grow wings that promise to carry me to this new freedom,
directly into the Heart of the Great Mystery.

*The Final Carryon Project was initiated by Fritz Roth, a Funeral Director and Grief Counselor from Bergisch-Glabach" (near Cologne, Germany), who died in December 2012. His son, David Roth, hopes to carry on his father's mission to help people accept death as a natural part of life that need not be hidden from view.

Change Across the Lifecycle

*W*hile for many years I've managed to live in denial of the steady progression of my "maturing process," now, in my mid-sixties, I face this change with a mix of wonder, denial, horror, anger, joy and bargaining behaviors. These poems invite you to explore your relationship with your progression of years and the changes that result, regardless of what age you are:

- Butting Heads
- Snow White's Mirror
- Summer's Time Keepers
- Backyard Hot Tub in December
- The Ways of the River Trail
- Where Time is Calling Me Now

Butting Heads

My daughter's school kept goats.
Being the Harry Houdinis of the animal kingdom,
the young kids escaped to run wild through
the kindergarten, sharp hooves tapping on linoleum,
leaving screaming children in chaotic bliss in their trails.

One spring morning while admiring the kids
standing on their mothers' backs, butting heads,
the math teacher dropped by, noted:
"The oddest thing. We built a bigger, improved enclosure,
transferred them over, only to discover it empty this morning,
the goats innocently lazing around their old pen."

Laughing, I felt vaguely disturbed,
recollected the changes I've stealthily escaped,
only to return to my old familiar abode.

At 60 (and more), I'm
butting heads with aging's encroachments,
my inner eye staring back on the old ground of youth.
I confess,
I want to move back there in the cover of night.

My soul is a frisky, leaping kid goat,
intolerant of confinement, ever-curious
and out for another adventure,
even as my body transforms into the tired used-up pen,
promises eventual release
to an even greater freedom beyond.
Perhaps by then,
I will know how to gracefully make the move.

Caryl Ann Casbon

28

Snow White's Mirror

They say that everyone is crazy
in some way. I can tell you my
diagnosis upfront. I think I am fat.
Like the Evil Queen in Snow White,
I gaze into the mirror, freeze at the sight
of an old witch no one else sees
staring me in the eyes with her malicious grin,
holding out a big red apple.
"Here, honey, eat this poison,"
and I do, go under the spell of
a strange slumber,
a distorted self-image in my heart.

What happened to my feminist Superwoman,
ready to challenge the culture's diminishments?
Why do I waste my time on images?

In futile resistance to my
up-and-coming minority status of old age,
I go vegan, guzzle green drinks,
ride endless miles on a stationary bike
watching the Dr. Prince Charming Oz of daytime TV
lure women with thin medical facts,
new potions, the tempting apple of long life.

The mirror's image never changes, only cackles back,
points out with a crooked, wart-covered finger
the new brown spot by my eyebrow,
stirs up insecurity reminiscent
of adolescent years with a body in change,
now in reverse, in decline,
my pants getting tighter each day.

By now, I suspect there is no Prince Charming to
awaken Snow White.
Perhaps I should just cover the mirrors,

Summer's Time Keepers

Time and light dance in summer,
waltz and extend the days with elongating sweeping movements,
then, slowly slowly spin and turn them back
towards darkness, so soon.

The backyard clocks summer's progression
with grasses, at first bright delicious green blankets of hope
giving up their worms to robins.
Then, slowly slowly bakes them into golden straw,
crunchy under foot.

Early June, the pond's frogs croak robustly until 3 a.m.
their lusty mating belches of desire,
then grow silent by mid-July.
In August their tiny offspring appear,
begin a brave solitary migration across the porch,
hopping towards deeper waters and muddy depths
to bulk up on insects, to winter through.

I mark time by watching my daughter,
who marries this year,
then calculate my mother's age when I first wed
to realize I am now older than she was
on that hot June day long ago.
I see Mom's smiling creased face clearly,
don't think her so old now,
nor different than me.
I, too, migrated from home,
searching for waters to call my own,
just as my daughter will do, must do.

They say time is not real in heaven,
but here we must reconcile
with its exacting ways.

Caryl Ann Casbon

No longer green or even golden,
I now seek Deep Time,
not scattered nor spent on busyness or trivial pursuits,
but focused and quiet, unbound to clock or season,
where the next poem finds me,
bubbles up from the deep waters I've moved towards
all my life.

Backyard Hot Tub in December

West winds gust
off the ice fields of Mt. Bachelor
as steam rises from the tub,
freezing stinging needles on my arms,
hot and cold extremes, both
stimulating and painful,
oddly unnerving.

The work of winter,
exposure to the wild, to the cold,
taking the needles directly to the skin,
diving towards inwardness, seeking warmth
in the Cauldron that holds me.

The air stills;
snowflakes silently appear like magic,
innocent ice babies
floating slowly downward
catching on eyebrows,
melting on water,
blending in with the others,
ready for the changes:
to be admired, sanded, shoveled,
absorbed into earth.
Evaporate in the reverse journey,
an ethereal embrace of winter's dance
of death, impermanence.
Resurrection.

The Ways of the River Trail

For many years I've hiked this trail along
the icy Deschutes River,
carved by volcanic lava flows 350,000 years ago,
ancestral hunting camps burrowed in its cliffs where fires
warmed, protected the ancients from exposure.

I once sprinted, sweated, jogged
just one more mile along this trail leaving a cloud of dust,
oblivious to the blinking lizard doing pushups on the sunny rock,
or the offended Douglass squirrel stamping its feet in outraged protest
at the disturbance of its pine-needled home.

I've sauntered down this path with my daughter in tow,
packed along peanut butter sandwiches, green grapes in plastic bags.
I've watched her examine pollywogs,
study mating dragonflies glued together
as though one;
her prolonged shocked stare at a flattened snake
squished by a mountain biker, drying in the heat,
her first encounter with death.

I've trekked this way with friends
chatting excitedly about heroics at work,
brushes with cancer, aging parents, failures,
missing the scenery as we confessed away the miles.

Now, I mostly walk this trail alone.

Yesterday
a boatful of rafters floated quietly by,
carried effortlessly on the current,
the guide pointing out beaver dams, fishing holes.
Suddenly
a woman stood up, then doused the group with a bucket of water.
Screams of laughter filled the canyon

as they retaliated their way downstream,
erupting into a camp song as they
disappeared around the bend.

I marvel at so many ways with the river.
Pray: please Mother Father God,
let there be room in the raft for me.
That's how I want to go home.

Where Time is Calling Me Now

On a wildlife tour
off the old Russian fishing village of Sitka, Alaska,
a grey whale and her calf
took turns breaching 50 feet from our boat,
thrusting their massive hulks into the air,
then sinking back into the icy waters,
leaving behind silent wakes of foam and bubbles.

Why do they do this?
Perhaps swimming along sucking up tons of krill is just too dull?
For fun, exercise,
or to knock off barnacles...sneak peaks?
No one really knows for sure.

Finally, this pair trailed alongside our bow
puffing spouts into the air, then dove,
their flukes disappearing in a final wave goodbye,
not to be spotted again.
I yearned to grab their tails and follow them.

Maybe time is calling for
a breach from the waters
I've tread for so long
feeding on the krill of my labors.
Time beckons for a powerful surge
that knocks off old barnacles
grown from extreme submersion...then to
dive towards the deep-down things,
where seaweed forests shelter worlds of alien creatures
awaiting on the ocean's floor.

A place where the currents carry me,
and I can swim with the whale and calf,
at least until their next ascent for another surface breach.

CHAPTER TWO

To Live Inside an Ancient Rhythm:
Poems for the Inner Life

*M*y first memory of a "Felt Presence" springs from Christmas Eve, 1954, at Trinity Presbyterian Church in Pasadena, California. At four years old, I mysteriously found myself alone in the quiet, darkened sanctuary of the church before the evening service. The walls were aglow with white pillar candles. I stood transfixed, staring at the warm light, enveloped in love, completely at home. In my child's heart, in my whole being, I sensed then that the most powerful energy in the world was in this place, emanating, not from the candles, but from an Unseen Presence. This instigated a life-long love affair with the world of the Spirit, a longing for intimacy with the Divine, something I've come to know as a birthright, for everyone, everywhere.

While this love affair has taken some serious detours, been called many names, wandered down interfaith highways, its intensity, now, is only increasing with age.

I came to learn that however strong as the longing for connection to the Divine might be, it's miraculously matched by the Creator's desire to be in relationship with us. To speak with us, witness life through us, guide us, and co-create with us. But we must approach the Mystery first, which is why I include the word "Oracle" in the title of this book. Like the ancient Greeks, we must go to the Oracle to begin the conversation with the intention to receive direction, insights, and responses to our questions and prayers in an unfolding flow of steady revelation. We also need to acquire the native language of Spirit to interpret the exchanges, to develop an "oracular sensibility" for posing questions, asking for help, and expanding our capacity for intuitive insight and symbolic thought.

Over time, with much practice, it became clear to me the Creator speaks fluent metaphor, parable, song, and story, delighting in literary forms of all stripes, and appearing in many guises such as prophet, trickster, and keeper of secrets, guru, neighbors, animals, enemies, an ocean wave, children and friends. It willingly reveals the meaning of your sorrows, challenges, opportunities and losses, all in holy timing, when you are ready. What is given is meant for service to others, to bring light and goodness to the world. It makes demands on you.

Approaching the Oracle is the ultimate antidote to materialism, to functional atheism, where we literally believe only what we see, and act as though we are alone in this scary world. Instead, we invite a state of *gnosis*, meaning a direct relationship with, and knowing of God where we experience personal mystical revelation. I used to think that only mystics and psychics could access this voice, this direct contact with God. Now I know how wrong I was. It truly is for everyone.

The Oracle is everywhere, meaning that the Great Unseen is a shape-shifting, multi-lingual, vociferous and generous Source speaking through dreams, coincidences, signs, the natural world, omens, synchronicity, messages in commercials, books, well, almost literally through anything to anyone half listening. This kind of listening demands faith, presence, attunement, and courage to follow the guidance. If you act on what you receive, the guidance and grace increases in frequency and grows louder over time.

May the poems in this chapter attune you to your relationship with the gnostic in you, and deepen your appreciation for how much and frequently the Oracle makes itself known in your life. It is waiting for you to learn its language, align with its frequency, and sign up for a glorious, bumpy ride.

Section I: Finding Your Way to the Temple
It is my wish that the following poems invite you to reflect on "your way within" and open possibilities for inner life disciplines that will sanctify your life.

Section II: Everyday Messengers
These poems offer glimpses of a kind of listening to the everyday, everywhere of the world for the wonder, grace, direction, instruction and gifts being offered all of the time.

Section III: Spiritual Mentors
May these poems invite you into reflections on your mentors, and how they have informed, as Mary Oliver so beautifully wrote, "Your one, wild and precious life."

Finding Your Way to the Temple

*A*ll spiritual traditions acknowledge the need for disciplines, or a praxis, that which opens our hearts, minds and lives to the experience of the Divine Mystery. However, the demands and distractions of the modern world, which should never be underestimated, endlessly side track us from dropping into these deeper dimensions that feed our souls, allow us access to the Oracle, and live more awakened, connected, wholesome lives. While these practices aren't difficult to enact, they require time for solitude, silence, time in nature, and commitment. In other words, they are countercultural. When we fail to commit to these "sanctuary times" we are inclined towards reactivity and ego-driven choices that lead us into actions we later regret. We feel cut off from our deeper selves, the Divine, and others. This is the ultimate form of suffering, a form of spiritual starvation, even while in close proximity to a feast.

Every person must discover their own path to "dropping into the depths," to finding their way within for allowing room for a rich inner life. The benefits of regular practices are immense. As my beloved mentor, Maryellen Kelley reminds us, "What you sanction, sanctifies you."

May the following poems invite you to reflect on "your way within" and open possibilities for inner life disciplines that will sanctify your life.

- The Oracle Everywhere
- The House of Prayer
- Partnership With the Unseen
- Rainy Day Blanket Tents
- Advice from the Tent Cities
- The Good News

The Oracle Everywhere

In ancient Rome, if a citizen sought guidance
she'd walked into the town square,
stand still, eaves drop on random conversations,
then listen for messages buried in strangers' comments
she believed were sent to her from the gods.
There's a name for these missives: *cledons*.

No need for Delphi, burning bushes, or singing angels.
The Oracle is everywhere, really, the omens for your soul
delivered from the Elsewhere
through the book you are reading,
a song playing softly on the radio,
your first feeling about someone, a dream,
or an animal crossing your path.
When you attune, you've got your hand on the Live Wire,
know where to turn next.

Gene, an inventor by trade,
posed the same question before arising each morn:
"OK, God, what are we going to do today?"
Now that is a great question.

I don't know how he listened for the answers,
but imagine responses arrived as "downloads,"
intuitive leadings that informed his innovations.
He knew that co-creation is where the riches reside,
the inventions, gifts meant for the world.

Recently I asked, *What does my poetry need?*
then I twice saw a mother raccoon teaching her four cubs
to fish in our backyard pond.
I asked her my question, to which she replied:
"You must move quietly in the dark.
Keep your cubs together until they can survive on their own.
Feed them first before anything. Then shelter them from

humans, our worst enemy. They hunt raccoons for our tails,
consider us a nuisance, run over us on the street and
generally, don't like us."

The Oracle had spoken in my backyard.
Now I knew what to do.

In awe, I gave thanks, then vowed to
to keep asking Spirit questions,
for aliveness depends on it.

The House of Prayer

A deep winter silence enfolds these Saskatchewan hills
muffled in snow, frozen hard, stark white, like
giant snow cones,
marked by deer tracks and ghostly dark, barren trees.
Only white rabbits, visible in flashes of movement,
disturb the seamless white peace.

Wind blows dry powder off the roof,
swirls it in front of the window like fairy dust, then moves on,
leaving behind a profound stillness. It beacons me to
stop. Attend. Set a table for Silence.
It speaks loudly here.

Sheltered from the calendar
for just a day in this hermitage cabin,
I wrap the winter morning
around me like an old afghan, plain-knit by my mother.
I give thanks for this season that clears out excess,
sanctions rest.

The silence absorbs my neediness,
my agitation.

Like the hardy chickadees
swooping in for a landing at the bird feeder
my soul alights and rests in this house of prayer called
Silence, this home called winter solitude
where I find myself enfolded in a Holy belonging.

Partnership With the Unseen

To know how to wait for guidance
after asking,
just awhile,
like overnight,
for the clear voice of sanity
that floats in like mist,
a soft touch on the inner skin
of your knowing.

Partnership with the Unseen,
astounding Grace.
An apprenticeship to the Messengers,
singing a chorus of Intuition in your soul.
Divine Indwelling.

Caryl Ann Casbon

Rainy Day Blanket Tents

Like childhood's rainy day blanket tents,
dark and private, just big enough for you,
journals keep secrets,
your confessions whispered in the dark.

Like tent cities for the homeless,
their blank pages welcome all: your impoverishment,
humiliating admissions, shame and guilt.
No one checks your spelling.

Like the Hebrew's Tabernacle tent during their exodus from Egypt,
journals move with you, portable shrines for treks through the desert
on the way to the Promised Land.
They hold a story as long as needed
until you understand the plot.
When you shine your flashlight on
Grace & Mystery that touch your life,
no one mocks, "You're imagining it."
"It is a neurological trick of the brain."
All is sacred here, written on the scroll of your life.

It took stacks of journals and 20 years
to admit I couldn't stay married,
then another 15 to comprehend
why I felt abandoned from the start, how I abandon others.
Four journals contain the grief from my mother's death,
another ten the accounts of my father's slow decline
when the whole family disappeared with him.
All woven over time with snapshots of my daughter's childhood,
finding the love of my life at 50,
times I stayed too long in the shadow lands.

I rarely revisit my journals.

Please God,

may no one read them.
Burn them on my funeral pyre!
Reduce them to ashes in blazes of
cleansing flames.

Advice From the Tent City

You didn't ask for it, but
here it is,
some hard-earned advice from a lifelong, compulsive
Keeper of Journals.

If you hunger to move closer to the Mystery,
the Way is intimacy with everything,
especially your pain.
What you are trying to avoid is your next teacher
or your greatest obstacle.
Nothing need be wasted.

You will suffer from amnesia, often, repeat your destructive patterns
until the magic day when you get the point, and remember,
and change. Be gentle with yourself.

The planet's Great Recycling Center is death.
Befriend death and count on rebirth,
no matter how much grief you endure.

All gurus have feet of clay. Always, think for yourself.
Spiritual communities darken with shadows,
but can hold great light. We need them.
Give them a long rope.

Truth comes in pairs, opposites that
set up home in complexity and paradox.
Delighting in this is a sign of wisdom.

You are more loved than you can fathom,
held in the hand of the Creator.
In you is a spark of the Great Light that never goes out.
There is always help, if you ask.

My last piece of advice is this:

don't take my advice. It never works.
You have to find these things out for yourself.
Keep your own journal.

The Good News

It's probably no mistake
it happens every year.
Just as December's darkness deepens
we play a restless game of Trivial Pursuit,
then feel bitter about it.

We complain about the grief that wells up
over awkward turkey dinners,
disappointing, wounding family dynamics.
Or roam for hours through websites and malls
in fruitless search of perfect gifts, quick material fixes.
We prepare nostalgic re-creations
of Mom's special cookies, fudges, rich meals
that add frustrating inches to waistlines.
We feast on that which leaves us hungry,
sentimentally singing *Silent Night* Christmas Eve
after weeks of being anything...but silent.

As though a great fog of needy confusion descends,
we abandon the Good News to a remote cave
a far distance from our lives,
replaced with holiday frenzy,
with artificial candles substituting for Light.
The profound, radical message, that *we are beloved*,
inaudible.

The Good News:
when Christmas mornings'
endless substitutes of
stuffed doggies, bowls of candy, each other,
fade,
when we put away the decorations
and let the quiet back in,
behold. It's there, always, everywhere.

Nothing, no one, ever,
can substitute, nor take Its place.

Everyday Messengers

I read somewhere that healthy relationships entail listening to your partner 70 percent of the time, and talking 30 percent. Deep listening involves more than taking in words. We also must listen with our eyes and hearts to body language, to the silence between the words, the timing and emotions that surround speech, what is not said, and the Spirit and context that holds together the patterns in conversations. Listening is, well, a full-bodied art form. May these poems offer glimpses of a kind of listening to the everyday, everywhere of the world for the wonder, grace, direction, instruction and gifts being offered all of the time.

- A Full Moon Winter Eclipse
- Inside an Ancient Rhythm
- The Prophet of Deceleration
- The Peace Tree
- Primary Lessons
- Hot Tub in Autumn
- Brother of My Heart
- Living Outside the Walls
- Wintering through on the Seventh Hole
- Baggage Claim

A Full Moon Winter Eclipse

Wrapped in flannel blankets
we gaze up into the night sky,
anticipating the moment when Earth and Sun align
to erase all light from the moon,
enveloping us in darkness.

Just bit players, a planet and sun star against
a backdrop of black holes, space junk,
trillions of billions of galaxies
being born and burning out,
shooting out,
beyond comprehension.

We say the Moon is rising
or the Sun is setting,
when it's Earth that's spinning.
Night senses dulled by our focus on the day,
we seldom look up
except to observe the meteor showers,
or full moon eclipses.

Grasping a coffee cup for warmth, I watch as the
the moon's surface gradually
quarters, halves and transmutes into an
orangey-black mass of shadow.

Now suspended in primordial darkness
for what seems an eternity, the eclipse
holds the timeless promise of the dark:
the eventual return of the light.

Inside an Ancient Rhythm

I was very young with this energy signature of fear,
a grip of tension embedded deep in my gut,
brought in from Another Time.

It sounds like these clicking computer keys:

tap tap tap,
the clatter of a mind with the 3 a.m.
blah blah blahs of small worries.
Like unanswered emails,
their blue warning dots demand response,
jarring me into a wide awake nervous fret.

Or: Drip drip drip,
the inner water torture of endless to do lists
inciting a harried rush from this-to-that,
fueling an addiction to activity that keeps me
on the surface of things.

Or the rapid, reactive:
thump thump thump
of a heartbeat when feeling
insulted, afraid, or threatened.

Tap, drip, thump escalate to:
boom boom boom
with Big Worries,
a tribal nervous system of pulsing fears:
disappearing bees, polar bears, ozone.
Wars, so many wars.
The seductive, deafening noise of these times.

Sometimes, beneath this cacophony
a Gong is heard.

Here, deep, prolonged fog-horned crescendos
summon my soul,
intoning, "You are so much more than this.
Return to Me. Rest in Me."

You could be ready
to live inside an Ancient Rhythm.
Let me ring you home.

The Prophet of Deceleration

Driving south over Mt. Shasta early one summer morning,
with no whale-like RV nor long-haul truck slowing me down,
I savor a blissful taste of freedom, when all seems possible,
like the day I left home for college.

Speeding round a corner,
the dread sign confronts:
Road Work Ahead
threatening, in bright orange,
Fines Double in Work Zones.
My heart sinks, knowing the gods of delays,
those who repair things,
are in charge of my journey now.
I must obey or pay a heavy price.

Turning off the engine,
I study the tanned unshaven Rotator of Signs
smoking a cigarette hanging loosely on his lip.
I speculate what his life is like, standing all day breathing tar fumes,
exchanging endless wordless encounters with strangers.
I observe a slow-moving dump truck lumber down
the middle of the road, think, "I'm trapped, doomed."

Rolling the window down, I feel the sun warm my cheek.
Breathing the crisp mountain air, I notice
butterflies alighting on roadside weeds, crickets chirping.
The quiet relief of the silenced engine settles me.
Uninvited questions seize my attention.

What on my road of heavy travel needs repair?
What double fines do I pay in my work zones?
What was this place like before roads?

This Sabbath moment granted by the
sign-bearing Prophet of Deceleration

ends when he suddenly rotates the sign from stop to slow.
Traffic moves again as he waves us on.
Trees and flowers blur as I accelerate,
the memory of crickets and questions
left behind with the car's exhaust.

Caryl Ann Casbon

The Peace Tree

An aged Eucalyptus tree stands rooted in enormous silence at
the center of a Peace Garden built around her massive bulk
for Sadako Saski, who was two and a half years old
the year the Atom bomb imploded and dropped on Hiroshima.

Fountains burble nearby.
Colorful origami cranes dangle from her branches,
enfolded prayers for reconciliation in their wings.
In Japan some believe if you form 1,000 cranes, your wish comes true.
Sadako completed 646 before dying from leukemia.

The eucalyptus' pungent, cat-urine-like scent permeates the garden.
Its oils harvested for stuffy nose remedies contain
the seeds of her destruction by rendering her highly flammable.
For this reason, some consider this giant a threat to peace.

I sit on the roots, mostly hidden below dry, rocky ground,
and vibrate with the tree's humming life-force,
feel her breathing, cleansing the air.
Imagine this subterranean cosmos of stems
anchoring her through drought and storm,
intertwining with other trees' roots,
keeping soil in place.

Is this where Peace abides?
Peace is surely here, or nowhere at all.

Today, a steady plume of radioactive nuclides blow
through her branches, leaking from Japan's Fukushima Plant,
carried in the jet streams to our shores.
Our lives are not so far removed from Sadako's after all.
Her classmates folded the remaining
353 healing prayers after she died.

People still send fresh origami cranes to hang
in the branches in the Peace Garden.
On wings of Hope we carry on.

Primary Lessons

During Show & Tell, I accidentally dropped
a dead gopher in a jar in front of the kindergarten class.
Its little body landed limply on a pile of glass shards,
my first memory of wanting to die, right there.

I almost quit school in sixth grade
when the teacher assigned dissection of live frogs.
The boys gleefully stood in line awaiting their turns
as I hatched a failed plot to save the amphibians,
then hid in the bathroom in horror facing the unnecessary,
cruel sacrifice of nature. Education can get it so wrong.
It is elemental whom you entrust your learning to.

Cute Bill gave me a St. Christopher necklace by the swing sets.
It meant we were going steady, but we never exchanged a word.
It was root beer brown, sparkled its promises in the sun.
I remember hanging upside down on the monkey bars
and kids laughing at my exposed underwear
back in those days when girls couldn't wear pants.
Primary love lessons, a muddled mix of secretive joy and shame,
loss of innocence, botched communication.

We're tested on the playground of relationships
right from the start, where the limits of loneliness and love,
violence and kindness bruise and instruct.

Sometimes classmates help each other, compete,
and sometimes steal each others' lunches.
Most of us want to learn but some take hits,
get excluded from the team, drop out too soon.
We must keep prayer in school.

Hot Tub in Autumn

Cold dark autumnal air of night
threatens my primal sense of safety
as clouds cover the new moon,
then blow on.

I strip naked to the elements,
let the cold penetrate my skin
before slipping into the round belly
of the steaming tub.
The warmth instantly goes about its
cleansing job, melting away
the armor of the day,
the tight places in my back
where I held in my truth,
the light anxiety of others' energies
clinging to my skin.

Steam lifts, dispels, and evaporates
their fleeting impressions
as my gaze rises towards the Vastness,
a reminder of my place in things.

Forgetting the day and my smallness
now lost in the Incomprehensible,
I hear an owl thump her massive wings
gliding through the night
where she hunts and finds home in the dark.

Brother of My Heart

Gazing up at the stars, Brother Francis asked,
"If these are the creatures, what must the Creator be like?"
Like a mirror, he reflected to each living being
their shining goodness, their belongingness,
their place in creation.

To the birds, to the worms, rabbits
 and honey bees, he taught,
"What you do gives Glory to God."
To ants, who never sleep, he urged them
to cease working so hard.

To humans, he disturbed.
His example evoking a longing for an
unencumbered, nonviolent, awakened life,
others transformed in his presence.
He taught to live like fly fishermen,
with license to catch and release,
but never possess.
In the lepers, worship the body of Christ.
If you want to follow his way,
place your naked feet on these stones:
humility, devotion, reverence, service.
His life was his sermon.
He is a hard act to follow.

Brother Sun, Sister Moon, all creation a family;
our lives can be instruments of peace God plays through our souls.
What we seek, we must first and finally, give away.
Holy, holy, holy.

Living Outside the Walls

The medieval-walled city's cobblestone streets
team with tourists speaking Dutch, Chinese,
gawking at monks in brown robes.
Uniformed youth groups cue in front of pizzerias,
or stare at the mummified body of Francesco Bernadone,
who stripped naked, shucked off his Crusader armor
and his parents' merchant life to live outside Assisi's walls.

On a pilgrimage of longing to feel his presence,
we slept in a pension just yards from the Porziuncola
where he rebuilt a crumbling Catholic church.

I awoke from a terrifying nightmare where
SS soldiers hunted me through narrow winding streets.
The church ramparts now haunted me.
The frozen smiles on gift store statues appeared sinister,
betrayed the dark European narratives entombed in
the walls and confessionals:
the Black Plague, the Grand Inquisition,
the German occupation of WWII,
all visited darkness upon this ancient city.

Yet even with the endless Crusades
and the Church's corruption,
Francis found Love outside the walls.

His spirit does still linger, whispering
...*where there is injury, let me sow pardon.*
When the church is lost, make new bricks.
Live outside the walls where Spirit can find you.

His imprint from another dark age,
not much different from today,
a testimony to the way of freedom in this world.
Holy, holy, holy.

Caryl Ann Casbon

Wintering Through on the Seventh Hole

Jogging past the neighborhood golf course,
acres of groomed, shaved turf
now stiff, lifeless straw under winter's solid hold,
I'm startled by a herd of female elk silently huddled together,
huffing steam clouds into freezing air.

A peaceful congregation of giants,
these warm brown muscular creatures nibble Juniper tree bark,
surrounding their young in a protective circle.

The sentinel lifts her nose to smell me.
What does she whiff? Laundry soap, deodorant?
I inhale a pungent, musky-earthiness from
mounds of scat covering the seventh hole,
usually reserved for tailored golfers.
The elk still tread their pathways
where only the ghosts of ancient forests now remain,
making their way around edges
of subdivisions, parking lots, health clubs.

In a synchronized movement they lift their heads, staring at me.
The sentinel lets out a honking, otherworldly warning,
then they gallop swiftly, like a flock of birds in fluid formation,
to amass at a distance.

Later, I search for the herd but they have migrated south,
not to appear again this winter. The pyramids of dung gradually
disintegrate into the lawns with the melting snow.

I long to see them,
yearn to belong, impossibly, to the world they carry,
hope they will return again with next year's snow.

Baggage Claim

Have you noticed lately how friends
get tight-lipped when someone mentions the word
God, as though blasphemy had been uttered?

Like a beat-up, unclaimed duffle bag on an airport carousel,
after traveling great distances, the word circulates round and around
as though it contains something too dangerous to handle,
too ragged to grasp, or impossibly small to hold its promises.
It's a word that carries, well, baggage.

Yet we sense a flight plan being drawn by a larger Presence,
Its fingerprints all over our souls, Its hands touching all creation.
We half-remember we've been around this carousel
many times before.

We spot our own imprints on the map,
roads that enticed us towards edges:
the open sea, certain difficult people, big mistakes.
We peer deeply into our shadowed canyons.

When silent, an unseen Otherness guides our thoughts,
reveals directions for the next move.
If pursued, we might discover something
original, uncharted, and the meaning of our detours.

Perhaps this is the new religion,
a creation story emerging in real time, where
the prophets are our neighbors, children,
friends; the scripture written is on our hearts.

At the final destination, a little weary from
so many delays, fattening airport food, now, frequent flyers,
we drop off all baggage,
traveling light with simply a ticket for the Reunion in hand.

Caryl Ann Casbon
66

Spiritual Mentors

*O*ccasionally, a person appears who changes the course of your life, who teaches you lessons that are fundamental to your growth, calls you to your growing edges, sees deeply into your soul and potential, and who, finally, offers the gift of friendship and love to you. An opening to a larger world is their gift and Grace in your life; destiny binds you. While this chapter could be filled with poems that include my husband, many friends and teachers, famous people who don't know me but who have profoundly impacted my spiritual formation through their writings, I choose to honor two people here who I have been blessed to know and love, true Anamcara, soul friends and mentors: Parker Palmer and Maryellen Kelley. The last poem, *Walking Like Pearl*, serves as a tribute to the many feline teachers I have cohabited with over the years (12 cats and counting), who are mentors to the natural world, Masters of the Present Moment.

May you be drawn into reflections on your mentors, and how they have informed, as Mary Oliver so beautifully wrote, "Your one, wild and precious life."

- The Man With Two Last Names
- Breakfast at Moby Dick's
- Walking Like Pearl

The Man With Two Last Names

The first time I met this gangly, mid-western Quaker,
I thought, "At last, a teacher of questions!"
How do you listen to the voice of the soul?
Who are you, and Whose are you?
His call, to live the questions, to live
—divided no more.

Fierce defender of the inner life, he opines: the soul
reveals her substance in the seasons' cycles, and thrives in silence.
It's *never* a waste of time to nurture your soul, but he cautions,
she cares more about your growth than safety, image or success.
She loves it when you take a risk.
He urges you to:
—welcome the wild animal of your soul.

Cracking himself up with goof-ball jokes fit for middle school boys,
he quotes old saws from his father:
Remember, Parker, today's peacock is tomorrow's feather duster.
If you spot it, you got it.
He points out:
—you teach who you are.

Parker weighs in on his Wisconsin winters,
the dark nights that almost extinguished his light.
When depressed, *you don't have darkness, you are darkness.*
The seeds of your future gestate in this place,
if you make it through.
He encourages you to:
—let your life speak.

He cautions that when you seek light without darkness,
it is artificial, like yellow neon lights in a garage,
so different than sunlight on an icicle at dawn.
No matter how grueling, strive to hold the tensions,
and sometimes create them.

Caryl Ann Casbon

Listen sincerely to others' stories:
—then stand in the Tragic Gap.

At the peak of intensity in a Hopi Indian Sun Dance
a clown appears, unexpected, shocking,
tossing candy at worshipers,
disturbing the ego's attachments.

At end of the day, Parker Palmer leads
the sacred dance in a circle
where Truth and trust are found in the Spirit within us,
among us, through us, wherein dwells
hospitality for the unknown Self, the unknown Other,
where he urges us to realize:
—the Word made Flesh.

Breakfast at Moby Dick's

In pink and grey early morning sunlight
the car curchunks
over wooden slats on Stearns Pier's splintery surface,
home of Moby Dick's restaurant;
we peruse the ocean for dolphin fins, seal heads,
the real treasures of Santa Barbara.

Fishing boats breast the waves heading out of the harbor.
The feast begins when Maryellen Kelley
envelopes us in bear hugs, then scans our energetic bodies.
She names our souls' desires,
then pushes us to consult what time it is in our lives,
what wastes time, and of course, urges us,
by all means, to have a good time!

She assigns us names: Holy Rascal,
Poetess, Warmie H, Suzie Girl.
She loves to make up words too.

In her company memory whispers,
"You've been with her before
in an ancient Greek temple,
a Celtic monastery in Ireland
or South American jungle
when women were shamans,
healers, mystics."

To the table she invites the Ancestors,
visitors from her dreams: bossy, bilingual,
authors from the Spirit World
speaking the language of Wisdom's Ways:

> When you are really mad at someone,
> picture their sleeping face.
> What you sanctify sanctions you.
> When you let go, don't discard.

Caryl Ann Casbon

She writes these sayings in books for them.

Prehistoric pelicans approach for landing overhead,
their big old bird bellies exposed as they descend.
We reluctantly prepare to depart,
new poems and prayers in hand,
knowing we are loved, blessed,
seen through to the core.
Asking, "How did we get this lucky?"

Walking Like Pearl

When the conditions are just right
Pearl pokes her old brown Balinese nose out
the front door,
freezes in a stance of indecision
then gently proceeds.

On ancient brown arthritic paws
she cautiously pads into the garden,
looks back over her shoulder,
then advances five more steps.....
freezes. Sniffs the air.
Licks her front paw.

Pearl studies the bushes,
rubs her whiskers on a stray
branch, then sits down
and blinks into the sun.

Eventually, noiseless light steps carry her forth again
in her feline-alertness, whole body attendance-
presence in nature.

People pay good money
to learn to walk like this.
I watch Pearl,
apprentice myself to
her pure cat wisdom.

A Guide for Readers & Group Work Design
Reading *The Everywhere Oracle* With Others:
A Guide for Soulful Engagement In Community

*I*f you wish to create a book club, design a retreat, share with a friend, a women's group, a men's group, a spiritual group, or just invite a casual gathering of couples that seek ways to engage through deep listening and soulful explorations with each other, this book is made for you! The poems and questions will invite you into a dialogue with their themes as they intersect with your inner life, and the process outlined below offers a way to begin the conversations and hold the space.

In 35 years of designing and leading groups of all stripes, I've learned about how essential it is for groups to have clear leadership and boundaries that are faithfully adhered to or people can hurt one another. Since these poems invite a personal level of exploration on a soul level, it is especially important that these boundary violations be avoided. Below is a structure, based on the Circle of Trust® approach, developed by Parker J. Palmer and the Center for Courage & Renewal. These instructions offer clear guidelines for how to be together to ensure respectful listening, safety, confidentiality and honest sharing as groups explore the poems together.

Leadership: I recommend one person, or a two-person team, lead the group, become familiar with and follow this simple but disciplined format to keep the group within safe boundaries. If you meet over a long period of time, the leadership can eventually be rotated. The leader's role is to follow the format, keep time, and gently guide the group back to the defined process when the group goes off track. The leader fully participates in the group and shares their reflections as would any other group member.

Group Size: The ideal size of the group is between 6-12 members. The larger the group, the more likely you will need to divide into smaller units to ensure adequate time for sharing. If you choose to meet with larger numbers, organize into dyads or triads. Keep in mind that the larger the group, the more leadership, skill and coordination will be required.

Frequency of Meetings: It is of course up to the group to choose how many poems to work with. If the choice is to work with only one or two poems in the collection, a single meeting will suffice. If a group chooses to work through all of the poems, a regular meeting schedule might be the best approach. The poems can be read in any order, and may also be used selectively in retreat or other briefer meeting settings.

What group members need to bring: Each person will need a pen and journal or notebook in which to write responses to the questions that accompany each poem. It is recommended that everyone bring a copy of the book so the leader need not photocopy the poems and questions. **It's highly recommended** that group members commit to faithful attendance to all of the meetings to ensure continuity. Growth of trust can build over time when not disrupted by absences and lack of commitment. Of course, legitimate interruptions occur, and there is always room for Grace for understandable absences.

Touchstones for Creating Safe Space: When you participate in a group with the goal of personal or spiritual reflection, you ideally enter a covenant with each other to be faithful to how you listen to one another, share, and most importantly, hold what is shared in confidence. Based on my 20 years of work through the Center for Courage & Renewal facilitating the Circle of Trust® approach, I recommend the Touchstones on page 77, which serve as "rules of engagement" during your time together. Take turns reading each Touchstone aloud at the beginning of every meeting.

Caryl Ann Casbon

Timing: Depending how long the group wishes to meet, choose one to two poems to read aloud, and then offer at least twenty minutes for silent reflection and journaling about the poem based on the questions in the Appendix. Since this is a soulful process, less is more. The timing should always feel relaxed and not rushed, with space for welcoming silence when no one is sharing. Also, be sure to begin and end the group in the agreed-upon times. This helps you hold to the boundaries, build trust, and encourages people to show up on time!

Sharing: After writing responses to the questions, if you are a small group, the leader invites whoever wishes to share to speak into the small circle. Sharing is never mandated. Individuals can always choose to listen and not talk about their writing (as so aptly put in the Touchstone, "This is not share or die."). You never march around the circle and demand that someone speaks, but allow people to speak when they feel ready. The leader makes sure that everyone who wishes, gets a chance to share. If someone goes on too long, gently say, "We need to move on so that everyone gets a chance to speak."

When an individual speaks: In this format, we listen respectfully, but do not comment on or debate what the person says. Unlike a traditional book group, this sharing comes from a personal response. There is no "right or wrong" answer to what the poem means, but only each person's truth or story about what they heard in the poem or question, and how it leads them to their own experience and insights. If this guideline is violated, the group will quickly become unsafe, and the sharing will remain on the surface.

Ending the group with a closing circle: Once everyone who wishes to do so has had the chance to talk about their reflections, the leader will end the session with a closing circle. This gives the participants the opportunity to state **briefly** what insights or surprises they experienced while reading and reflecting on a poem, or while listening to one another. When this is complete, you may end the session by rereading the poem you explored that day.

An Outline for the Group Process:

Below is a format for structuring a group based on an hour and half meeting time.

1. Welcome: The leader welcomes the group and can invite a brief check-in before starting to reflect on the poetry. **Note**: be careful or this can use up a lot of time.

2. Touchstones: Read aloud the Touchstones, and if you wish, discuss them and how they might be speaking to, supportive of, or challenging for each of you.

3. Reading of Poetry: If you are starting a new section of the poetry, for instance, the Inheritance section, begin by reading the introduction to that chapter and/or section for an overview. The leader reads aloud the selected poem, then asks someone else to read it aloud again.

4. A Time for Reflection: Invite the group, in silence, to write in their journals for 15-20 minutes in response to the questions for the poem (in the Appendix section). People are always welcome to respond to their own questions if they are more meaningful to them. They may also choose to respond to only one of the questions. Some may choose to draw, make a list of thoughts, or simply sit and enjoy silent reflection during this time.

5. Sharing in Community: After the 15-20 minutes of writing and reflecting, invite sharing into the large group. For a larger group, divide into dyads or smaller groups. Remember the Touchstone, "This is not share or die." People are always welcome to pass if they do not wish to talk. When someone talks, we simply sit in silence and give full attention to listening to what is said.

6. Closing Circle: As a closing, invite anyone who wishes to share, briefly, in a sentence or two, what insight they are taking away from the group. End the session with rereading the poem or poems you worked with that day.

For more about the trustworthy group process: This group design is a simplified format of a circle of trust process as outlined in *A Hidden Wholeness: The Journey Toward an Undivided Life*, by Parker J. Palmer (1), and developed, cultivated and loved into life by an international community of facilitators prepared by the Center for Courage & Renewal. If you wish to deepen your understanding of the use of circles of trust, I recommend you not only read *A Hidden Wholeness*, but visit the Center for Courage & Renewal website at www.couragerenewal.org to find opportunities for retreats, programs, online resources, and further involvement with this program.

Touchstones® for the Everywhere Oracle Group Process

- *Extend and receive welcome.* People learn best in hospitable spaces. In this circle we support each other by giving and receiving hospitality, both to what comes up from within, as well as what is shared in community.

- *What is offered in this circle is by invitation, not demand.* This is not a "share or die" event! During this meeting do whatever your soul calls for, and know that you do it with our support. Your soul knows your needs better than we do.

- *Speak your truth in ways that respect other people's truth.* Our views of reality may differ, but speaking one's truth in a circle of trust does not mean interpreting, correcting or debating what others say. Speak from your center to the center of the circle, using "I" statements, trusting people to do their own sifting and winnowing.

- *No fixing, no saving, no advising, and no correcting each other.* This is one of the hardest guidelines. But it is vital to welcoming the soul, to making space for the inner teacher. When someone speaks in this meeting, we simply listen and receive their sharing in silent attendance.

- **When the going gets rough, turn to wonder.** If you feel judgmental, or defensive, ask yourself, "I wonder what brought her to this belief? I wonder what he's feeling right now? I wonder what my reaction teaches me about myself?" Set aside judgment to listen to others—and to yourself—more deeply.

- **Attend to your own inner teacher.** We learn from others, of course. But as we explore poems, stories, questions and silence, we have a special opportunity to learn from within. So pay close attention to your own reactions and responses, to your most important teacher.

- **Observe deep confidentiality.** Nothing said in this meeting will ever be repeated to other people.

[1] Palmer, Parker J, *A Hidden Wholeness: The Journey Toward An Undivided Life*, 2004, John Wiley & Sons

Created by the Center for Courage & Renewal
www.couragerenewal.org

Caryl Ann Casbon

Reflection Questions

CHAPTER ONE
Where Time Is Calling You Now
The Alchemy of Change

Section I: Inheritance

A Toast to an Empty Garage

1. When you read about a "bomb" from the past waiting to go off, does anything come to mind about your own life? What is your first response to this poem?

2. What name would you give to a "clutter zone" in your garage that is not current with who you are now, or perhaps even holds you back? Do you need anyone's permission to cleanse it?

3. Is there something in your life that needs to be cleared out, donated to Goodwill? If you did so, what might it make room for?

Hunger: Where Can't Turns to Want

1. Create a list of some of the "mantras" you were raised with. Can you identify their origins? Whose voice chants them in your mind?

2. Is there a "habit of mind" you learned in your family or culture that is difficult for you to break?

3. Is there one "mantra" you fear you will take to your grave? Is there one you have managed to outlive?

The Year I Give Up Alcohol

1. Can you identify a habit in your life you admit has significant influence (i.e., overworking, spending, busyness, dieting, talking, eating, exercise, etc.) on you? Spend some time describing it, then ask this habit some questions:

   When did you enter my life? How did I acquire you? What

are you doing here? Exactly how often and how long do I engage with you?

2. What metaphor comes to mind that captures this habit's essence?

3. When you imagine giving it up for a year, or "living without this shell," what do you think you could discover about yourself? What support would you need to attempt this change, if you wish to make it? What do you hope might come from it?

One Generation Off the Farm

1. When you consider your parents' lives, is there something you value, miss, or yearn for that you are "one generation" removed from now?

2. What has been lost, and what has been gained with this change? Can you imagine, or do you desire a way to reclaim a quality of this now?

3. Imagine a "fierce beauty" you long to apprentice yourself to. What would that be?

Section II: The Crossroads of Change

God's Holy Mirrors

1. How does this poem speak to you regarding your own healing journey/journeys?

2. If you were to circle a holy well with a wound at this time in your life, what would it be? How did you incur this injury, and how long have you carried it?

3. If you circled the well in the direction of illumination, what would you hope to glimpse in your reflection as you drink from the cold waters of self-knowledge? How many trips might this journey take?

Dummy's Guide to Outsourcing Morale

1. When you look back on "morale problems" you've had in the past, how do they typically show up in your life? What symptoms appear?

2. If you were to name a "morale" problem right now, what would it be? What would "outsourcing" this problem look like? How could you "insource" it?

3. Ask your morale problem some questions you would rather avoid, and see what it has to say to you.

The Harm Reduction Program

1. Can you identify some aspect of yourself that at times wants to do "harm," either to yourself or to others? When does it most often appear? Does an image or metaphor come to mind when you think of it?

2. If you were to treat this aspect of yourself like a feral kitten, to be brought in out of the cold, how could you go about this? What do you think might happen if you did?

3. Are there qualities to this instinct that are useful? What name would you give it? What does "peace" mean to you in relation to this quality?

Crossroads of the Emergent Self

1. When you read this poem, does a "shape shifting" time come to mind from your own life?

2. Make a list of the "crossroads of the emergent self" moments in your life, where you experienced noticeable shifts into new forms, new levels of consciousness.

3. When you study this list, what patterns exist in these shape-shifting experiences? What paradoxes and tensions do they reveal?

4. When you reflect on your own death, what shape do you imagine might emerge out of the ashes?

The Four Directions for an Awakening Edge

1. Is there an "awakening edge" or question you sense about your life right now for which you wish to ask for help? Are you ready?

2. What would your prayer be for your question?

3. What "fruits of the spirit" would you want to sift through in relation to your question?

4. Where might you seek strong light and support for wisdom in exploring your question?

From the Perspective of Eternity

1. In what ways do you seek and find support and clarity from others when you are on "thresholds of change"?

2. Can you recall a time when the right question or a fresh perspective changed your life? How did it come to you?

3. What in your life now could use "the perspective of Eternity"?

The Final Carry-on

1. What do you hope to "ride out on" as you leave this life?

2. If you could pack a carry-on for this crossroad called death, make a list of what you would put into it, and why.

3. When you consider this final transition, what do you imagine greets you "on the other side"? Looking back on your life, what do you think you will see?

Section III: Change Across the Lifecycle

Butting Heads

1. How would you describe your relationship to the age you are right now?

2. What would soulful aging look like in your life? Do you know anyone who is a model for this?

3. When you read about the metaphor of a soul being a wild adventurous kid goat, does an animal come to mind that captures the nature and essence of your soul? Perhaps you would like to draw it in your journal.

Snow White's Mirror

1. When you look into the mirror, what does it reflect back to you about your aging and body image?

2. With the progression of the years, what aspects of yourself do you fear losing?

3. In what ways, if any, do the culture's diminishments impact you?

4. As you age, what do you sense you need to relinquish, and what do you think you might be gaining?

Summer's Time Keepers

1. What sort of "time keepers" do you have where you track the progression of your life's seasons?

2. What time is it now in your life?

3. What quality of time does your soul yearn for?

4. Describe the places where you find "Deep Time," unbound by clocks.

Backyard Hot Tub in December

1. Is there any unnerving "work of winter" to be done in your life at this time?

2. Places that need exposed?

3. What "cauldron" holds you through your winters?

4. What does winter teach you about life and death?

The Ways of the River Trail

1. Where on the trail do you find yourself in this poem?

2. Is there a repeated activity that has been there through the different stages of your life, that you use to mark your life's progression? A holiday, outing, practice, vacation, etc.?

3. If you were to mark these stages of your life, what names would you give them?

4. Complete this sentence: "This"_____ is how I want to go home."

Where Time is Calling Me Now

1. When you read this poem, what "waters you have traveled in for a long time" come to mind? Do you find yourself longing to swim differently?

2. Do you know any guides who might direct you in this new direction?

3. What would a dive towards "the deep down things" look like for you? What strange sea creatures might you find there?

CHAPTER TWO
To Live Inside an Ancient Rhythm
Poems for the Inner Life

Section I: Finding a Way to the Temple

The Oracle Everywhere

1. When was the last time "the Oracle" spoke to you in your "backyard"? What was the message? Who was the messenger?

2. Can you discern a pattern to the ways you generally look for and receive guidance?

3. Is there a question you would ask to receive guidance for today?

4. If you were to say a prayer each day, before getting out of bed, what would it be? What does "aliveness" depend on in your life?

The House of Prayer

1. If you could set a table for silence in your life right now, sheltered from your calendar, what do you think silence would say to you? How much silence do you actually invite into your life?

2. Is there a place in you that could use winter's clearing, something that needs to be put to rest? Is there a dark-

ness in you that could use tending, befriending?

3. Describe your "house of belonging" where you can find shelter for your inner life. If you don't have one, where might you seek it?

Partnership with the Unseen

1. What does the phrase, "A partnership with the Unseen" mean to you?

2. Is there a place in your body where you experience this partnership?

3. Has there been a time recently when you were aware of "astonishing Grace" in your life? Create a list of "Astonishing Grace Moments" across your lifetime.

Rainy Day Blanket Tents

1. What in you is homeless, seeking shelter? How would you describe this in the privacy of your journal?

2. How would you answer the question, "What or where is the scroll of my life?" Do you have a place that is entirely safe and sheltered for your secrets, a record of your inner life? (Perhaps you don't keep a journal but instead take pictures, write letters to a close friend, etc.)

3. If you were to pick up a journal right now, is there a story in need of storage in its "Tabernacle," where you could carry it long enough for it to reveal its meaning in your life?

Advice From the Tent City

1. Is there "advice" in this poem that speaks to you at this time?

2. For a change, write your own poem, starting with the opening line, "You didn't ask for it, but here it is, some hard-earned advice…"

The Good News

1. When you read "The Good News," what does it evoke for you about your own experience with the high holidays of your tradition?

2. If you were to name the "substitutes" you tend to pursue, what would they be? What are they substituting for?

3. When you consider your spiritual heritage and traditions, what are some of the positive contributions they make to your life?

Section II: Everyday Messengers

Full Moon Eclipse in December

1. If you were to describe your "night senses" what would you say about them? How often do you spend time watching the stars? What do you discover when you do?

2. What promise does the dark hold for you?

3. When you try to imagine the scope of the universe, what is its impact on you? How does it inform your sense of self, your relationship with Mystery?

Inside an Ancient Rhythm

1. If you were to name the most dominant rhythm of your life, what would it be? Perhaps a certain song or dance captures it.

2. At what speed limit do you drive your life?

3. Try to give sounds to the different rhythms in your life throughout your day and night, and tie them to images if possible. How do they feel in your body?

4. What, if anything, "rings you home," calls you to live "inside an ancient rhythm?" What is it like in there when you begin to live inside of this rhythm?

The Prophets of Deceleration

1. Is there a "god of delays" slowing you down in some way right now? Describe what you are noticing in this stalled-out place.

2. When you read, "Fines Double in Work Zones" how does that speak to you on a metaphorical level?

3. When the roads of your life are in need of repair, after a few blown tires from heavy use, how do you go about making repairs? What sort of delays might be required?

The Peace Tree

1. In your life, what serves as a symbol of peace? Describe it in as much detail as possible. If you wish, sketch this symbol, and reflect on what is has to say to you.

2. What seeds of destruction might this symbol contain?

3. What threatens your own sense of peace? What restores it?

Primary Lessons

1. When you look back on your education, what is your first memory of encountering something very wrong that created a moral dilemma for you? How did you respond?

2. Did you at any time entrust your learning to an untrustworthy teacher or educational program? What did you learn from doing so? What does make for a trustworthy teacher?

3. What are some hard, "primary" lessons you recall about your early relationships? What stories would you tell, if you wrote this poem?

Hot Tub in Autumn

1. Where in your body do you "hold in your truth?"

2. If you were to "slip into warm waters" for cleansing, what in your life could use purification?

3. Is there a place where you find home in the dark?

Questions for Reflection: Brother of My Heart

1. If you were to identify a longing in you, what name would you give it?

2. Is there someone you wish to follow in their ways? What would that require of you? What would the sermon of your life be?

3. What do you seek that you must ultimately give away?

Living Outside the Walls

1. If you were to sojourn on a pilgrimage at this time in your life, where would you go, and what would you be hoping to find? Who or what has gone there before you?

2. Is there a saint, mystic, or spiritual teacher who speaks to you in a significant way? What do you admire about him or her and their teachings?

3. What does "living outside the walls" mean to you? What would that require of you?

Wintering Through on the Seventh Hole

1. When you read this poem, in what ways does it speak to you?

2. If the elk could address us, what do you think they would say?

3. Is there some version of an "elk herd" that you follow in your neighborhood? Describe your relationship with it, and what it teaches you.

Baggage Claim

1. What name or names do you give to the "Unseen Presence" in your life? What makes this language native for you?

2. How has your understanding and experience of the Divine evolved over time?

3. Complete this sentence: "This _____ is my new religion."

Section III: Spiritual Mentors

The Man With Two Last Names

1. Chose a line from this poem and write about how it speaks to you.

2. Are there mentors in your life for your spiritual journey, your inner life? What do these mentors teach you?

3. If you were to become a "fierce defender of your inner life," what would that look like in practical terms?

Breakfast at Moby Dick's

1. Who in your life makes you wonder, "How did I get this lucky?" when you depart from them?

2. How does this poem speak to you about the qualities of a mentor?

3. When you think about mentoring others spiritually, what do you imagine offering them?

Walking Like Pearl

1. When in your life do you experience this quality of presence and attention to nature, or anything else, for that matter?

2. Do you have any master teachers from the animal world who show you the way? Where do they take you?

3. Ok, give it a try. Go outside and walk like Pearl. Then return and write about what you experience!

Acknowledgements

*W*hile writing by nature requires a form of hermitage, of isolating oneself to nurture the emergence of ideas, images, stories and words, for me, it is not a solitary journey. I have been handed many slender threads of Grace through support, lovely and loving listening, advice and encouragement along the way, both in the seen and Unseen worlds. These brief acknowledgements are profoundly inadequate, but, nonetheless, express the spirit of sincere gratitude to each dear soul who has accompanied me along the way:

Jesse John Casbon, my life partner, the love of my life, who loved my poems before I could even hear them. Maryellen Kelley, my spiritual mother, for without her recognition and boundless support of my "poetess" nature and potential, I would never have had the courage to write this book. My dear friend, Ruth Shagoury, the most creative person I know, who recognized me as a writer from the beginning, and conspired with me to teach and lead with imagination and joy. Nancy Cleary, who through her invitation to publish my book, and her creative genius with design and her overall support, manifested what still feels like a miracle to me. . .my first book of poetry. My precious daughter, Paige Ann Cloke, who assists me in negotiating the exciting world of the social media. My friend and mentor, Parker Palmer, who taught me about the power of questions, and the beauty of being "alone together" in soulful community. Claire Lucas, who offered her keen intelligence and careful eyes to proofreading the book. Ken Saxon, who early on offered to sponsor a poetry reading in Santa Barbara before the book had a name. Shelli Macintosh, who introduced me to my publisher. Anne Selby, who took my photos through the lens of the Angels. Sharon Palmer, Karen Sue Maunder, Nancy Gump, Carol Ferris, Jim Rogers, Susan Plummer, Howard Wittausch, Terry Kemple, Polly Jacobson, Jan Christian, Mary Bowers, Joanne Cooper, Nancy Edmundson, and Georgia Noble, Doug and Phillip Casbon, and many more friends who listened and encouraged me along the way!

Caryl Ann Casbon

And, finally, to Aunt Betty, who, from the perspective of eternity, doesn't give a rip about those antique glasses.

Index

Notes

Notes